Around Kirkham

IN OLD PHOTOGRAPHS

A Fylde 'character', name unknown, seen in Poulton and Kirkham in the 1890s.

Around Kirkham

IN OLD PHOTOGRAPHS

Collected by
CATHERINE ROTHWELL

Alan Sutton Publishing Limited
Phoenix Mill · Far Thrupp
Stroud · Gloucestershire

First published 1994

Front cover illustration: A Fylde 'character' in
the 1890s

Copyright © Catherine Rothwell 1994

British Library Cataloguing in Publication Data

A catalogue record for this book is available
from the British Libary

ISBN 0–7509–0647–2

Typeset in 9/10 Sabon.
Typesetting and origination by
Alan Sutton Publishing Limited.
Printed in Great Britain by
Redwood Books, Trowbridge.

Contents

Kirkham Club Day in 1905.

Introduction

Since 1066, when its church was already in existence, the ancient market town of Kirkham has witnessed a long pageant of history. Situated in the heart of Amounderness, later the parliamentary division of Fylde, its system of government gave way in 1894 to an Urban District Council of nine, ending the medieval sway of the Thirty Sworn Men. Kirkham's chief landowners, the earls of Derby, the Butlers and the Cliftons and the mill owners, the Langtons, the Shepherds and the Birleys, all had great influence. By the 1920s Kirkham's railway station was important, its mills were so busy it assumed the title 'cottonopolis', and the surrounding rich farmland was earning an enviable reputation for cheeses.

This was in direct contrast to a century before when Cragg's cart, 'a vehicle with springs covered with bands and canvas', passed through Kirkham carrying passengers from Preston to Blackpool daily, though only twice a week in winter. The Fair Trader, pulled by a single horse, reached Preston while a coach-and-pair from Preston is on record as being 'a matter of wonder and astonishment'. The Fylde Union Coach travelled at six miles an hour, the only excitement being 'old coachman Barnett's dash downhill from the top of Preston Street. No doubt wonder grew when a Preston & Wyre Railway engine was worked between Kirkham and Lytham by local men John Sanderson and Tim Southworth.

Stirring tales came out of the Civil War in Lancashire. The Birley Arms became known as The Red Heart because of battles fought in the lanes of Kellamergh. Bloody Looan (Green Lane) was the scene of a fight between Lord Derby's men and Cromwell's soldiers who, like the Romans before them, used the ancient ford across the Ribble near Guide's Inn. For a time soldiers terrorized the neighbourhood but, left to themselves, villagers went the even tenor of their ways: hand-loom weaving, peat cutting or grazing cattle. It was during the Civil War that 'A declaration of a strange and wonderful monster born in Kirkham' was printed throughout the land. Mrs Houghton 'a Popish gentlewoman' who gave birth to a deformed baby, had been heard to say that she would rather bear a child with no head than a Roundhead. The Revd Fleetwood and Colonel More decided that all should know about this 'manifestation of God's anger'. Strangely enough, another wonder, the birth of a two-headed calf on a Kirkham farm was announced in the *Fleetwood Chronicle* in 1845.

Murders were not always solved. Peg Hall, a serving girl, was found with her throat cut, and ever afterwards her ghost dressed in a linsey petticoat and white bed gown haunted the Crofts near St Michael's church. The ghost of a young man was seen several times near Treales at a spot where the scent of rue filled the air, 'a plant well known to the wise to spring up of itself where blood has been wilfully spilled'. Indeed in the nineteenth century the district was famous for its ghosts. Spectral

Bloody House (Thatched House Tavern) was so named because it was close to Kirkham's gibbet.

The first issue of the *Preston Evening Guardian* on Monday 25 July 1870, price 1*d*., reported how an old man in Kirkham was cured of gout. A chimney was being swept and the sweep's boy walked the roof to take a bird's-eye view. He returned via the wrong chimney, terrifying the old gentleman. As the boy made good his escape up the chimney the black urchin cried: 'My master's coming for you,' whereupon the old man fled the room as if the Devil really was after him, his gout cured by fright.

The Clifton papers reveal much: fines imposed for brawling, keeping evil company, unlawful gaming, dyeing hemp in the house and not bottoming the ditches. Will Townend was paid 8*d*. a day for 54½ days' work on ditching.

'The Great Sicknesse' which raged in the 1620s spread from Poulton to Kirkham: '. . . the first that dyed was the wife of Thomas Watson, 27 June 1631.' The Thirty Sworn Men eventually became strict about all the dung in the streets: each householder had to cowrake (sweep) before his own door. They could also be understanding, providing 8*d*. for sugar to 'refreshen' communion wine, relief for widows whose husbands were slain abroad and relief to John Osborn, a Russian merchant robbed of £10,000 by pirates. Perhaps this led to nineteenth-century sarcasm: 'Kirkham road is the road for tramps . . . pauperism made a pleasure by the workhouse.' Against stiff opposition implementation of sewering was finally passed in 1849.

From old residents it is clear that customs prevailed into the twentieth century. Oak Apple Day was observed by wearing a sprig of oak leaves; anyone who forgot was chased and whipped with stinging nettles. There was the custom of Riding the Stang, Soul Caking and the saving of a Steen of butter until March to help the family through a difficult month. Another tradition, recognized as legitimate, was roaming the villages to beg flour, eggs and milk for making pancakes and puddings on 10 October after old Michaelmas Day.

Certainly Kirkham had its share of characters. One saddler presented his bills in rhyme. After repairing the harness of a traveller riding horseback to Blackpool in 1842 he wrote: 'To cutting and contriving, hammer, nails and driving – three shillings.' Indefatigable Ellen Smith did washing for the Birleys, bore fifteen children of which twelve survived, including triplets which were put on show in Blackpool, and she was known to ride horseback to Fleetwood. Men's societies in Kirkham included the Independent Order of Oddfellows and the Fylde Union Lodge of Freemasons Number 533, which was moved to the Fleetwood Arms in 1844 under a dispensation.

Sailcloth, at first hand woven in cottages, was later manufactured in the linen and flax spinning mill of John Birley & Sons from raw materials imported via Wardleys, a port then almost as busy as Liverpool. The advent of steamships and the railway inevitably brought a decline in demand as 'King Cotton' was in the ascendancy. By the nineteenth century Kirkham became a mill town. Whittle & Turner Weaving, a family business established in 1909, had 212 looms four years later. Progress Mill, established in 1915, expanded to 684 then 900 looms, employing 280 workers including weavers, labourers, sizers, knotters and drawers. Producing high-quality fabrics, they later pioneered weaving in new fabrics: nylon, terylene, velveteen collar cloths, bonded cloths and gaberdines, one of which won a gold medal at the California and Sacramento Exposition of 1959.

Mr Hollis formed the Sunnybank Weaving Company in 1924 with a thousand looms. His premises were requisitioned in 1940 during the Second World War but they reopened in 1946. It was he who launched the Jacquard Weaving Company with eighty employees and sold his furnishing fabrics as far away as Australia. To 'Old Barnett', the coachman, it would have been 'a matter of wonder and astonishment'.

SECTION ONE

Kirkham

Five views of Kirkham in 1920.

The early seventeenth-century parish church which was replaced by the present one in 1822. On the right is a thatched Fylde longhouse where the parish bier may have been stored. To the left is the old burgage house. The old church was said to be 'a cold cheerless place on Sundays in winter, not warmed in any way. People had to endure the service almost perishing with cold.' At this time Revd J. Radcliffe was headmaster of the grammar school and curate in charge of the parish church. Revd Dr Webber, vicar at Kirkham, in the days of pluralities 'took some £1,200 a year from the parish for travelling from London or Ripon to preach about once in a twelvemonth'. The erudite Revd J. Radcliffe's sermons were not understood by the average Kirkham parishioner and although he liked to teach bright boys, the slower ones were left to his head boy to handle while he went off with his gun. He was said to be 'a capital shot'. The Revd J. Radcliffe was also involved when new. rulings were made for the grammar school, apparently the most influential trustees being members of that ancient London Guild, the Company of Drapers. A special meeting was held at the Black Horse Inn in 1835 to settle this matter. The Revd R. Clegg, the 'cantankerous vicar of Kirkham' in the seventeenth century, threw Cuthbert Harrison of Bankfield out of this church, disagreeing with the latter's Nonconformist principles. To support his family, Cuthbert 'practised physic' most successfully, medically attending local gentry and his own numerous children.

A bronze shield umbo, found at Dowbridge, Kirkham, one of many artefacts of Roman origin that have come to light since the early 1800s. It was sold for 30s. and is now in the British Museum. Mr Willacy who discovered the shield in a crushed state in Mill Hey Field also reported evidence of 'mossy chiselled red sandstone foundations', possibly part of the Roman fort. Red brick tiles, burnt bones, pottery, charred wood and bricks emerged in abundance, having been protected by the curve of the River Dow, giving evidence of Kirkham's past. A Mr Loxham found an urn containing bones and an iron amulet in 1840, and nine years later, during brick-making operations, twelve urns filled with burned bones were discovered. In 1985 Mr Eddie Green of Dowbridge unearthed what looked like part of a Roman wall. Fragments of Roman and pre-Roman pottery continue to be found on raised land. Time is now of the essence for the present Lancaster University Archaeological Unit dig, because bungalows are to be built in the area. It is possible that a recently discovered ditch surrounded the Roman fort on Dowbridge or it may have been a boundary ditch around the civilian settlement outside the fort. The mansion Carr Hill House was built on part of this site.

Edwin Waugh, who journeyed through the Fylde in 1861. He met many characters on the way: William Garlick who wove 'pow-davey' (sail cloth), a lark catcher who used two milk pails, a collector of salt-water snails, and watercress gatherers. His writing reveals a rural scene: 'Lizzy churning in the dairy; Granny baking and Little Tom, the cow lad off early with a cart of coals.' His recently discovered verse to friend Samuel Laycock is full of delightful humour. At that time Samuel Laycock was a photographer, which explains the verse written in Lancashire dialect.

> If thou want to tak' th' picher o' me
> I'd be proud on't owd crayter – but then
> Thou has my heart now, dosta see?
> Thou connot tak' that o'er again.
>
> But th'odd bits there is on me – well
> Good luck to thi pickterin craft.
> Thou may pike what thou like for thysel.
> Thou'rt welcome to what there is left.
>
> Get on wi' the pickters owd mon.
> This morsel o' life's rayther tough.
> There's not mony posts that con
> Get a livin' by takin fooks off.

The old Swan Inn, Poulton Street, towards the end of the nineteenth century. This thatched inn with a porch to keep out draughts resembles many other inns and houses in the town of long ago. On the west side of Church Street was the site of the Blue Bell Inn near to where Dr Lewis lived and, previously, Dr Parkinson. The old Swan was a posting house when John Armstrong was innkeeper in 1892. Certain inns throughout the country were used for collecting letters when the mail coaches called. Another of the three posting houses in Kirkham was John Singleton's New Inn, the other being the Post Office Inn, passed daily by Jack Cross, Town Crier of Kirkham, with his clanging bell. When Kirkham was the busiest and most important town in the Fylde it had thirteen taverns and nine beer houses. The lady on the left is wearing a crinoline skirt.

Kirkham's church is of ancient origin. The first one, built of wood, was possibly on Carr Hill but since Norman times it has occupied the present site and was the ecclesiastical centre of fifteen vills or townships. Mentioned in Domesday Book as Chircheham, the parish stretched from the River Ribble to the River Wyre (33,564 acres). In 1093 it was given to Shrewsbury Abbey by Godfrey, sheriff of Count Roger de Poictou, and in 1280 it was among the possessions of the Abbey of Vale Royal. Following Henry VIII's massive Dissolution, on 11 December 1538 St Michael's was given to his newly founded Christ Church, Oxford together with the rectory and whole manor of Kirkham, plus the chapelry of Goosnargh. In 1872 part of the demesne lands and some rights were purchased by Thomas Birley but the Dean and Chapter of Christ Church still hold the right of presentation of the benefice. The records of the Thirty Sworn Men make reference to church improvement: 'two shillings and one farthing for a whip to whip the dogs out of church'. This photograph was taken in 1932.

The office of the Fylde Waterworks Company, seen here in 1910, was purchased on 10 November 1870. Originally owned by the Hornby family, it was later a savings bank. A large iron door from a strong room was removed from this building, taken to Blackpool and used by plumbers to hammer lead on.

Freckleton Street in 1900 showing weavers' cottages with cellar windows where hand looms were placed for maximum light. Tall chimney stacks and the mews area of an inn where coachmen changed horses are features of old Kirkham. The notice reads: 'good stabling – Bowling Green.'

The original Birley's linen mill, built in 1861 and photographed in 1900, is on the right. At different periods other buildings were added as the business grew. By 1892 it was reported: 'A good deal of trade is carried on at the extensive flax-spinning establishment of Messrs John Birley & Sons.' The lamp (right) is where apprentices rang a bell on Shrove Tuesday.

This Lancashire & Yorkshire Railway locomotive used to steam through Kirkham railway station. The Preston & Wyre Railway opened in July 1840 with stations at Maudland Bank, Preston, Lea, Kirkham and Fleetwood. On the day it was installed in 1846, introduction of the electric telegraph led to the capture of a defaulting steamship passenger.

Thomas Langton Birley of Carr Hill House, son of Thomas Birley of Milbanke, who was the first chairman of the Fylde Waterworks Company. He is here photographed in 1902 when he was a director of Fylde Water Board. Another important townsman connected with the board was Dr Thomas Shaw, son of Miles Shaw, who was born at Bolton Houses, Treales, in 1815 and went to Kirkham Grammar School. In his medical training Thomas studied at Dublin Hospital, the Dublin School of Anatomy and at St Thomas's Hospital, London. Returning to Kirkham from London on one occasion, the coach lost its way in snow and took six days to reach Preston. Dr Shaw set up a partnership with William Knipe in 1838 and lived at Harvey House.

Shepherd House in Preston Street, Kirkham, was photographed shortly before demolition in January 1957 to make way for a garage showroom and offices. This beautiful building, similar to the home of Roger Charnock Richard, the enterprising Kirkham merchant who built the Station Hotel, was not considered worthy of saving. Although it was one of the town's three protected buildings, the County Planning and Development Committee declared it not of sufficient architectural value. (Courtesy of *Evening Gazette*)

John Leyland Birley examining his first model locomotive in the grounds of Milbanke in 1903, with his daughter and possibly Mrs Jane Leyland Birley alongside. The engine was invented and built by him, as were many other models, in his workshop in the mansion erected by Thomas Birley in 1808. The wide open view across to the now-demolished flax mill should interest people who live on the present Milbanke Estate. This thoroughly well-behaved engine did not need a penny spending on it in ten years. 'Besides being used for pleasure trips it transported soil from the estate,' reported the *Model Engineer*. The extra height of the cab was designed for comfort. The influence of the Birley family on the town of Kirkham, coupled with that of the Langton and Shepherd families, was considerable. From 1868 Messrs John Birley & Sons made linen and sail cloth for Admiralty orders. Ships from Wardleys carried their wares as far as Russia, and Baltic merchandise came to Kirkham on return journeys.

A locomotive designed by John L. Birley in 1893. Mr John L. Birley, known locally as 'Johnny Leyland', had his own model railway in the private grounds of Milbanke. For convenience he had a private door from Kirkham station leading to his grounds which were adjacent to the Lancashire & Yorkshire Railway. The track extended 400 yd along two sides and engines, carriage sheds, sidings and even a small platform were built. Mr John L. Birley, assisted by his gardener, laid the 20 in gauge track. The Birley family were such benefactors to the town of Kirkham that it is of interest to recall anecdotes connected with them. The Revd John Shepherd Birley was much esteemed as a magistrate (in the 1840s the largest room at the Post Office Inn was used for Petty Sessions) and shortly afterwards Mr Willam Birley succeeded him. 'What sort of a magistrate do you think I shall make?' he asked a Kirkham workman. 'Well, Mr Birley, you'll send 'em to th'House of C'rection and before they've getten to Clifton, you'll send for 'em back.' 'Do you think so John?' was the mild reply from the man who was father to Edmund Birley of Clifton Hall, also a magistrate. Edmund became Mayor of Preston. Another Birley, Mr Henry, turned night into day, preferring to work during darkness and to spend daylight hours as something of a recluse. The Birley dynasty was linked with the Langtons. John Langton, favouring Oliver Cromwell's cause, was the first of the Langton family to settle in Kirkham and founded a charity school in the town in 1760 to clothe and educate forty girls. A Kirkham lady, Ann Hankinson, joined him in this venture.

A coachman with trap and four horses drawn up outside Milbanke, *c.* 1870. This Georgian mansion was built by the Birley family who were mill owners in Kirkham. After A.L. Birley's death in 1877, Jane and Edith Jane lived on there. The hall was demolished in the 1930s. An Ordnance Survey map dated 1843 calls the house Mill Bank.

The Fylde Institution with military hospital photographed by the Preston publisher Evans, *c.* 1915. Known also as The Guardians' Institute, it was built at Wesham in 1906. The First World War kept the military hospital busy.

Mr John L. Birley's windmill, 1903. Needed for pumping, this was of his own design. When a firm quoted £40 for making one he decided to build one himself. The materials cost less than £10 as most were on hand in his own workshop. It was an appropriate addition to Windmill Land. (see p. 66)

John Leyland Birley, born in 1857, and photographed some twenty-two years later standing beside his penny farthing bicycle when he was an undergraduate at Oxford University. Already his interest in mechanics was evident. He went on to design a steam launch and model locomotives besides those illustrated.

Kirkham's favourite corner in 1890 with lamp (the first street lamp was lit in 1837), circular fish stones and Jackson's seed and guano shop. The pony and trap from leisurely days when people had time to exchange pleasantries evokes the nineteenth century. The men would discuss harvest, cattle feed and animal cures. Food, children and fashions for forthcoming events occupied the ladies: 'duchesse hats in white felt, green plush Princess poke bonnets trimmed with swansdown, mob caps, the fashionable coaching hats trimmed with black velvet, muffs trimmed with beaver or violets'. One milliners shop in 1898 had designed 'a large white picture hat with white plumes and orange blossom . . . this for a wedding next week'. Mrs C. Butler of Clegg Street had a centre-piece in her window, 'a beautiful basket with roses, berries, mistletoe, ivy – the latest styles, French and English, prevail in this establishment'.

Aspinall's Enamel in sevenpenny tins produced in one hundred colours, was sold in Kirkham in 1889 and thereabouts 'for beautifying everything' in cottages, farmhouses and stately homes. A small booklet *Valuable Botanical Remedies* dating from the same time came to light during the renovation of an old Kirkham cottage. It included a cure for toothache: 'Dissolve camphor in a dram of nitre and add a few drops of ammonia.' Anti-cholera powders contained Peruvian bark and tormentil among other unlikely ingredients.

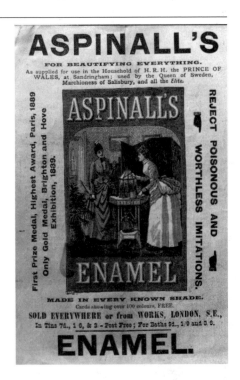

John Hesketh, photographed *c.* 1900, who farmed at Cardwell's Farm, Treales was an orphan brought up by the Heskeths of Moorside Farm who taught him farming skills. He knew how to improve harvest yields and was a regular caller at Thomas Jackson's Fylde Guano and Seed Establishment (selected seeds and guano manure were originally imported via Skippool and Wardleys). Mr Charnock Richard, the pioneer in guano importing, had been in demand for his veterinary skills since the 1840s in what was predominantly an agricultural area depending greatly on horse power. 'He did much, not only for the prosperity of the town but for the Fylde District.'

A typical town scene in Kirkham of the 1870s. Clarkson, baker and confectioner, advertises on one gable end, a carrier's cart is delivering outside the Co-operative Wholesale Stores, and a tired horse and trap approaches from Town End, having climbed the hill with two passengers. Otherwise there is scarcely any traffic in an area now laden with cars and lorries. On the right the spire of the Congregational church can be seen. A long-gowned lady by the lamp finds her bicycle useful, but the scene in general evokes a leisurely pace of life. The traditional market became obsolete but three cattle fairs held annually continued for many years. Every Christmas Day a football match was played in the streets until Queen Victoria stopped this boisterous custom. A fire in 1810 destroyed the Moot Hall (Town Hall). A room in the upper storey reached by a flight of stone steps outside the building had been used for flax dressing. On the large floor below, town business was conducted by the Thirty Sworn Men. By 1825 manufacture of sail cloth, cordage, and fine and coarse linen was in full swing, soon to be followed by the manufacture of cotton. One of the oldest relics known in Kirkham, still extant, is at the bottom of the hill as you enter Kirkham from Town End. In the form of a wooden medallion, J.E. 1729 is marked with a series of four Xs beneath a faded figure of a man with raised arms. This very old street sign for Curriers is thought to have referred to The Curriers Arms.

'The Ancient Town of Kirkham Welcomes Your Majesties' refers to the visit of King George V and Queen Mary in July 1913. Always a loyal town, Kirkham is proud of its ancient lineage. The largest and most important Saxon parish in the area of that day, it is one of the oldest ecclesiastical foundations in Lancashire. Its grammar school dates back to 1549, the oldest foundation in the Fylde. The archway was rich in royal heraldic shields, with the flags of all nations, especially the Union Jack. The residents could be proud of their effort, knowing that another arch, 'God Bless Our King and Queen', featured elsewhere in their town.

The royal train bringing King George V and Queen Mary to Fylde in July 1913 passing North Junction cabin, heading for Blackpool North. In the right background is Walton's Bridge; in the left background is the 'flying junction'. The track in the foreground is the 'new line' direct to Blackpool South. The Lancashire & Yorkshire locomotive (note LNWR stock) at this point is just level with allotments cultivated by Kirkham residents. The Royal tour started in Blackpool, the King and Queen travelling to Kirkham by road in either a Rolls Royce or a Daimler.

The old windmill, Kirkham, built in 1812, seen here *c*. 1900 in such a dilapidated state that one might believe the legend of the red-haired ghost of Kirkham windmill. Everything it touched with its hair burst into flames. One of the most intriguing sites for a windmill in all Fylde is this high point which was the Roman encampment, strategically important for its intersection of a ridgeway running east to west, part of the great system of roads devised by Roman engineers. The rivers Wyre and Ribble had fords for crossing but in between lay impassable moss lands. The line of villages follows the ridgeways: Lund, Dowbridge, Kirkham, Wesham, Bradkirk, Weeton, etc. The Romans used these ridgeways which were an extension of Watling Street. One from Ribchester passes through Kirkham.

'We're having a lovely time here', one of many picture postcards at the turn of the century reflecting the cycling craze. With the advent of the safety cycle, this quick and easy method of getting around was particularly popular in Kirkham and its surrounding villages. William Benson was ironmonger and cycle agent at 81 Poulton Street and in 1901 William Bennett was 'maker of the Fylde Champion Cycle'. The Seagull Cycling Club streamed through Kirkham many a time before the First World War.

A Queen Anne candelabra from among the treasured possessions of the light and airy parish church at Kirkham. This foundation existed in 1066 and is one of three in the Hundred of Amoundeness mentioned in Domesday Book. However, all except the tower and part of the chancel was rebuilt in 1825 at a cost of £5,000. In 1843 the tower was rebuilt and with its crocketed broach spire is 156 ft high. The stained glass window at the east end was presented by A.L. Birley and the eagle lectern is in memory of T.L. Birley. On 30 June 1892 Lady Eleanor Cecily Clifton laid the foundation stone of Christ Church, once a chapel of ease to Kirkham, in order to provide for the people of nearby North Wesham. It was consecrated by Bishop Moorhouse on 27 September 1894. (Courtesy of *Lancashire Evening Post*)

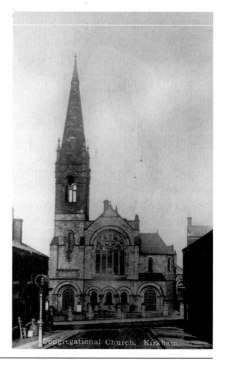

The Congregational church in Poulton Street, *c.* 1920. The foundation stone was laid in July 1896 and the church opened the following year. It is a handsome building which replaced the old Independent chapel built in 1793 and rebuilt in 1820. In March 1914 a Sunday school was opened in a building costing £3,500 which was the gift of Mr A.C. Bowdler, a former scholar and teacher. The church stands on the site of the Old Bowling Green Inn.

Ribby Hall was referred to by surgeon barber Hugh Holmes in 1873 when it was newly built as 'a large modern edifice embosomed in rising plantation belonging to John Hornby'. By the 1920s, about the time of this photograph, the Duckworths were the occupants. Disciplinarian and scholar, Mr Duckworth provided the lych-gate at Wrea Green church.

An old-fashioned winter in 1916 showing Kirkham's main street banked high with frozen snow. The horses would need their hooves wrapped in flannel to get a grip on this slope. 'Perfection Flake' reads the tobacco advertisement on Church Street corner gable end, identical to one in Poulton at that time.

A Club Day procession in Kirkham, *c.* 1902. The grandmothers of these girls considered it a treat to sit round the fire before bedtime, listening to ghost stories. One old lady recalled 'what a creepy feeling' when the tales ended and they crept upstairs to bed in darkness, afraid of their own footfalls.

Jim Willacy, now 86, is seated second from left on the fish stones, *c.* 1920. The town's lamp and fish stones remain Kirkham's focal point. It is interesting to note that Thomas Langton Birley paid for a gas lamp to replace the one moved from here to the corner of Freckleton Street.

Mr Ward, druggist and dentist, standing at the door of his shop on Preston Street early this century. As a chemist he also sold agricultural tools and veterinary remedies. Martell's Brandy and Orion Australian Wines are advertised in white ceramic letters on the windows of his shop frontage. The property, which was old even then, featured large cellars for storage. Old directories show that eventually the shop consisted of three adjacent premises made into one. In earlier days the site was occupied by Hugh Hornby's house, built in the eighteenth century, to which was attached a small thatched dairy. 'At the drug stores sovereign remedies are provided for almost every ill that the flesh is heir to' was reported in 1895.

Tom Gregson, cornet player and member of Kirkham Brass Band, was one who joined Kitchener's Army of Volunteers in 1914. He played with the band on Club Days in Kirkham and the villages around. D. Gregson & Company of 10 and 12 Poulton Street were drapers in 1892.

Kirkham Grammar School, on a postcard of 1920, was a free grammar school until remodelled by the Endowed Schools Commissioners in 1880. The buildings near the parish church were superseded by new ones in Ribby Road at a cost of £10,000. In 1926 the headmaster was the Revd Cresswell Strange.

This group outside the creeper-clad Kirkham Grammar School was probably photographed after a prize giving or speech day, c. 1930. It includes from left to right: Revd Cresswell Strange (headmaster), the Earl of Crawford and Balcarres, Mrs Strange and Revd W.T. Mitton (vicar of Kirkham).

'Kirkham Pleases Our Prince', a popular postcard from the 1900s when the dashing Prince of Wales, who later became the Duke of Windsor, was photographed by Arthur Winter of Preston. His Royal Highness passed through Kirkham in 1927. A very popular member of the royal family in the early days of the twentieth century because he was prepared to talk to the workers, the Prince toured the Fylde, inspecting war veterans. As the accompanying letter from Lord Stanley dated 9 June 1927 shows, detailed arrangements were made in advance.

A letter from Lord Stanley from 10 Upper Portman Street, London on 9 June 1927 in which he writes to confirm that His Royal Highness the Prince of Wales will be visiting the Fylde on 28 June and that he, the son of Lord Derby, would be there to greet him. The letter says: 'Will you kindly make the necessary arrangements with Mr Trubshaw, Chief Constable of the County'.

Mowbreck Hall, damaged by fire in March 1972, was at that time empty and had been for three months as its new owner planned to convert it into flats. Originally built in the twelfth century and rebuilt in 1732, this historic hall was once a hunting lodge for the Earls of Derby. For 300 years the Westby family, devout Catholics, lived there. In the 1960s it became an exclusive country club whose owner Kenneth Newby claimed to have seen the hall's ghost, a Roman Catholic priest, George Haydock, who was cruelly executed for his faith in 1584. Among the inhabitants in Kirkham who had to register as recusants were John and Thomas Westby of Mowbreck, Richard Richardson, Doctor of Physic, and John Swarbrick of Wesham. For non-attendance at the established church, recusants had to pay 'Sunday Shillings'. John Westby died in June 1722 and was buried in the Mowbreck chapel in Kirkham church. Thomas Westby of Thistleton who succeeded him was buried at Kirkham, so ending the Catholic tradition in the family in 1842. (Courtesy of *Lancashire Evening Post*)

Kirkham Cricket Club in 1936, with John Ball in the middle behind the shield. Second from right is Robert Hesketh. At this time the game was played on ground behind Mayfield Avenue near where Kirkham Library is now situated. These are Kirkham Grammar School boys.

Wesham Rose Queen, *c.* 1920. Tom Wilkinson is the kneeling page and John Hall the velvet-clad boy standing and holding the queen's train. All were ready for the long-anticipated Kirkham Club Day.

Preston Street in 1910 showing a traction engine and a shop on the corner of Freckleton Street advertising Cadbury's Chocolate and Quaker Oats. In the traffic-laden times of November 1990, Kirkham and Rural Fylde Rotary Club issued a certificate: 'This is to certify that the holder walked the Kirkham and Wesham By Pass prior to official opening.'

Clegg's the cloggers of Town End also had shops in Fleetwood, Poulton and Thornton. A hundred years ago clogs were universal footwear. Even the wood for soles was specially chosen. Later Clegg's premises became shoe shops as eventually the trade of clog making died out.

'Best of Chums' depicts five smart young men at Kirkham Camp in 1913. A contemporary popular postcard showed a soldier by a sentry box. 'I am on the look out for you at Kirkham Camp. Just raise the flap and you will find the views I guard are in behind.'

Officers of the 4th King's Own link arms at the end of a summer camp at Kirkham in 1912. Among the group is the chaplain. They were unaware that in two years' time the First World War would change their lives and greatly affect the famous Lancashire regiment.

Army farriers, horses and men in Kirkham during the First World War. A grand variety concert for wounded soldiers was held on Wednesday 22 November 1916 at the Co-operative Hall, Kirkham, admission 6*d*.

Some of the 4th King's Own in smart uniform and with eight drums at Kirkham Camp in 1912. Officers of the 4th King's Own Regiment were assembled for photographs on the same day.

Entry to the paddock at Carr Hill Races, Kirkham on 18 April 1938 was 5s. including tax. Developed on the site of Carr Hill House before the Second World War by Edward G. Sergeant, the area was sold for housing development after the house, for a time a restaurant and night club, closed.

The Lawns, Carr Hill Hotel, sited almost opposite Kirkham windmill, on a 1930s postcard. In 1920 Mr Penney purchased certain manorial rights and Carr Hill House, which after his death in 1923 were sold to Edward G. Sergeant.

Rose Queen Betty Hudson of the Congregational church on a Kirkham Club Day. Her train bearer is Alice Crook and the group is outside the manse which later became a nursing home. The Club Queen each year was chosen mainly on attendances at church and Sunday school and each church or chapel in Kirkham participated in turn.

St Michael's church choir included three ladies in 1905, when the vicar was the Revd Henry W. Mason. In those days there was a gallery in the church. The present organist and choirmaster is Mr E. Lees.

The camping ground used by the military at Kirkham in 1912. In the First World War it was particularly busy. In the background on the left is Wesham Roman Catholic church. At the end of the Second World War an RAF camp on land south of the new road was used as a demobilization centre.

Station Road, Wesham in 1907 when the lamplighter, William Wright of 10 School Lane, came round twice a day to the cast-iron, fluted gas lamps. Carriers' carts stocked up in Kirkham with twine, meal, 'physic' and snuff for the villages. The corner shop run by Thomas Towers, boot and shoemaker, was near William Gardner's Stanley Arms.

The Willows Roman Catholic church from across Ribby Road in 1932. Mentioned in Pevsner's *North Lancashire*, this building was designed by A.W.M. Pugin and is believed to be the first Roman Catholic church since the Reformation to possess a peal of bells. It is dedicated to St John the Evangelist and has a Lady chapel. The Chapel of the Holy Cross has a window with three lights described in Barrett's Directory of 1924 as 'gorgeous'. The centre light has a full-length figure of St Helena holding the true cross and the side lights are emblazoned with flaming cherubim. The ancient chapel serving the Roman Catholics of Kirkham was at Mowbreck Hall, but a chapel at the Willows was built in 1809. This was superseded in 1896 when the church was greatly improved. A large gilt statue of St Peter was added, the sanctuary opened, new statues of the cross erected and new sacristies designed by Pugin the elder. Father Sherburn, who had lived at the Willows for forty years and died in 1854, was the guiding hand behind these rich improvements. A Caen stone altar and the high altar, also of Caen stone, are brilliantly sculptured with richly gilded reredoses.

The horse-drawn ambulance used for Moss Side Isolation Hospital in the years before the First World War. Cases of scarlet fever were taken away from the community to prevent infection spreading. The hospital is now boarded up and is in a dangerous state awaiting demolition.

The result of the mill fire at Kirkham which occurred before the Second World War. Once the property of Henry Langton Birley, after his death the mill passed to Messrs Redmayne & Isherwood who used it for processing cotton waste, a flammable commodity.

A mill girls' party held at Whiteside's Mill in May 1937. In the middle is the 'Gaffer' and the girl second from left is Ann Crook. Celebration may have been in anticipation of Wakes Week in June when all the factories in Kirkham and Preston closed down. As early as 1841 there was a mill in Station Road, then known as Wrangway. Other noteworthy mills were Progress Mill in Orders Lane, Brook Mill, Selby Mill and Sunny Bank Mill, the last three being in the area of Sunny Bank. All were powered by the cheap coal brought to Preston and Freckleton. A 1922 directory lists eleven cotton spinners and manufacturers in the town. Mill chimneys were a feature of Kirkham landscape and early this century 'knockers-up' went round as mule spinning and other machinery started at 6 a.m. Birley's old flax mill in Mill Street became a rag mill, Moss's mill a biscuit factory, Selby Mill the site for Benson's Crisps and one small mill became a perfume factory.

A Kirkham Club Day with the Rose Queen under the flowered canopy and Margaret Ball at the front, c. 1930. In the background can be seen a Kirkham mill chimney. At this time Kirkham's mills numbered among them James Butler & Co. at Brook Mill and Walker Moss & Co.

A 1930 Club Day procession in the main street showing the many people involved in this annual event held on the second Saturday in June. Processions started in the morning and continued into the afternoon when the Congregational church joined in. The Willows RC church chose a May Queen and the parish church a Rose Queen.

The New Fylde Workhouse at Wesham, photographed soon after it was built in 1906, provided accommodation for 320 inmates, superseding the 1844 building. A workhouse was instituted in 1726 because there were so many paupers and the town was notoriously dirty. According to the minute books, the recommended cod liver oil and quinine were said by the guardians to be too expensive.

The Old Workhouse, Kirkham, fronting Moor Street, c. 1900. Its occupants were reduced by epidemics of typhus fever. It was replaced by children's homes for the Fylde Union from designs by Mr F. Harrison of Lytham. In ancient days this area had the duck pond and ducking stool for witches and scolds. Moor Street and Station Road were once moor and common land.

The Saint George Hotel in Station Road at Town End in the early twentieth century. On the right are the old premises of Bennett's, painters and glaziers, and Cleggs, 'the largest stockist of footwear in the district'.

A trip to St Anne's, *c.* 1909, showing the pier in the background. The Girls' Friendly Societies from Kirkham and Wrea Green found this a good day out. 'Ozone' was medically recommended for the mill girls – hence the boat trip – to combat tuberculosis.

An early 1900s bird's-eye view of Kirkham, giving an impression of layout when each householder had a farm, orchard and garden, with the land in strips. Long gardens show what were tofts and burgages. Towards the south, fields were known as old earths. Orders Lane is a corruption of Earth Lane.

Wesham church before the tower was added, with a group of children in white pinafores, probably assembled in the early years of the twentieth century for a Club Day rehearsal. The children carried decorated baskets and walked in procession amid silk banners. This was the high point of the year.

Kirkham Scout Troop, *c.* 1919. The troop met in Peter Ball's yard up Moor Street where horses were shoed by blacksmiths Joseph Fleetwood and Thomas Royles. Fourth from the left, by the drum, is Eric Ball.

Enthusiastic subjects wave outside Royle's and Hunter's Tea Stores on the occasion of the royal visit of King George V and Queen Mary in July 1913. The visit inspired many flags, bunting, draped lamp standards and two triumphal arches. The arch which read 'God Bless Our King and Queen' was in Ribby Road near the Willows church.

A 1902 postcard of Poulton Street with its cobbled pavements showing a thatched cottage on the left and two small girls wearing white pinafores. Roger Charnock Richard's house and premises are further down on the right. The old lamp adds atmosphere.

Ward's chemist shop is on the right of this Poulton Street postcard from the days before motor cars. The Congregational church is on the same side. Thatched houses on this side of Poulton Street were demolished in 1875 to make way for the Co-operative Stores.

The Old Bowling Green Inn at Kirkham in 1890. This thatched tavern with bull's-eye glass window-panes and shutters was a favourite meeting place for labourers when the railway was being built. Mr R. Redman was the innkeeper. Licensee Jim Reeder, interested in old inns, said in 1970 when he was in charge of what was once known as Royles Old Black Bull Inn in Preston Street: 'Every second house in Kirkham was a pub!' At the Live and Let Live there was a quoits club. Other inns in Kirkham parish were the Masons Arms, the Black Horse, the General Elliott, the Coach and Horses, the Black Bull, the Clifton, the Anchor, the Dog and Partridge, the Shaws Arms and the Packet Boat. Mr Roberts's tin plate shop adjoined the Old Bowling Green Inn. The whole site in Poulton Street was razed in 1896 to make way for the Congregational church.

Mowbreck Hall covered with ivy at the time the Windham Hales lived there around the turn of the century. In later years the creeper was stripped from the building. During the Civil War in this part of Lancashire it was noteworthy that provisions for Lord Molyneux's forces came from Mowbreck Hall.

Mr and Mrs Windham Hale in the late nineteenth century, who were for some years tenants of Mowbreck Hall. Mr Windham Hale, agent for Lord Derby, was an influential man in Kirkham life. He was presiding magistrate at local court sessions and Chairman of the Parish Council of Treales, Wharles and Roseacre in 1924.

Kirkham parish church bellringers, 1930. Front row, left to right: Tom Wignall, Bob Gibson, Victor Gibson, Tom Roberts. Back row: E. Townsend, J. Worthington, Victor Wheatley, Chris Cookson. The peal of bells was overhauled in 1922. In 1870 the sexton was John Wray who had to toll the bell, lay rushes and clean the leads.

A medieval stone coffin, preserved for many years in the tower of Kirkham parish church. Later it reposed on the path leading to the main church door but in January 1994 it was reported stolen. Records refer to this coffin and an ancient stone font.

Afternoon sunlight at 3.20 p.m. showing the spire of St Michael's church to clear advantage during the 1930s Depression. The men on the left were probably unemployed. Behind them is the corner grocers shop advertising Lyons Tea. It was decided in 1843 to replace the tower with a new one surmounted by a lofty spire. On a windy day, 21 November, Thomas Clifton of Lytham Hall laid the corner stone of the steeple built by public subscription. Considered a gala occasion, all the clubs in the town formed a procession, the mills stopped but the workmen were paid by the masters, 600 schoolchildren waved flags and there was a sermon lasting one and a half hours. Using a silver trowel, Mr Thomas Clifton buried a time capsule, while the rain came down in torrents. Three hearty cheers for the squire ensued, then it was off for roast beef and plum pudding in the schoolroom.

The Superintendent's House, Children's Home, Kirkham in 1921. In 1906 when the Guardians Institute was built at Wesham on the site of the original Fylde Union building, five children's cottage homes costing £10,000 were provided at Kirkham. At that time Fred Brown was clerk and registrar to the Fylde Board of Governors.

Poulton Street with the lamp in the centre denotes a Kirkham with its first Boots chemist and Hedges Brothers, 'the Great Boot Providers'. On the right of this 1906 postcard published by Rigby of Kirkham, at No. 113 is W.B. Roberts 'Wholesale and Retail Potato Dealer'. The cast-iron street furniture and massive stone walls have gone.

Church Memorial House, Church Street, in 1919. Previously called Ash Tree House, it was then the home of William Wright Shaw who practised medicine in Kirkham along with Thomas Shaw, Sidney Wigglesworth and Charles Court. Dr Thomas Shaw, who lived at Harvey House, died in 1893.

Gardens and cenotaph in the 1930s. The parish church is on the right and the 'Rec' (Barnfield Recreation Ground) is on the site of Cloyce Pasture, adjacent to the church. Cutting through the Crofts by the parish church was a recognized short way to Treales village.

Kirkham Police Station, 23 June 1965. An early police station was built in Freckleton Street, PC Crean being a very busy man dealing with fights and drunken bouts common in Kirkham. Thomas Butler was a well-known Kirkham constable in the 1840s, described in *Reminiscences of the Fylde* as 'a bricklayer who might be at work resetting somebody's oven when word was sent that a "feight" was in progress. Off went Tommy with his trowel in his pocket. He dived into the ring and marched off the combatants, meek as lambs, to the iron cage, next day to the magistrate and finally to the stocks.' Another character, Jobbing Jemmy, church warden and constable, put it into verse:

> Come lads disbust or else I must, shall and will engage,
> To put you in a kind of place they call the Iron Cage.

By 1901 Petty Sessions were held on alternate Wednesdays at the County Constabulary in Freckleton Street, Kirkham. By then there was a long list of magistrates eligible to preside. The 'iron cage' or prison in Kirkham was housed in the upper storey of the workhouse situated in Back Lane and any prisoner was in full view, so word flew quickly round the town. Most cases were poachers or drunkards but more serious malefactors were incarcerated in the Black Hole, a cellar in the Poor House. 'The name carried terror with it,' records one observer in 1883. (Courtesy of *Lancashire Evening Post*)

The Kirkham team of the Fylde Sunday School Football League in the 1950s. Headmaster Mr Hargreaves was trainer and supporter. The first Football Club was founded in 1860 some years after the Cricket Club.

A celebration held in the back yard of a Kirkham inn a few days after the completion of Blackpool Tower in 1894. Walter Smith, a ganger, is standing at the back, third from the left.

Thomas Appleton's shop at 55 Poulton Street in the 1890s. He was a wine and spirit merchant, as evidenced by the large oak barrel. The Co-operative Wholesale Society's Stores was next door and William Singleton, ironmonger and nail maker, was not far away. A tin-plate worker, milliner, grocer, furniture broker, saddler and clock maker were also along this stretch.

Kirkham Band assembled, perhaps for another Club Day, *c.* 1930. They had recently won first prize in the Duerden Challenge Cup. Mr Little is among this group. It is thought that the first man to be knocked down and killed by a motor car in Kirkham was one of the band members.

Kirkham Farmers' Discussion Society visiting Port Sunlight on 18 August 1936. This model village created by Lord Leverhulme of Lever Brothers was a place of pilgrimage for workers. The Kirkham farmers returned with tales of 'Prosperity Sharing' and of the garden city covering 220 acres with 700 roomy, cheerful cottages where pure air and perfect ventilation made for perfect health. In 1909 a co-partnership system was instituted under which every employee aged from 25 upwards who had served the company for five years became a partner. Swimming baths, gymnasiums, clubs for workmen and girls, a library, theatre, schools, allotments, ambulance corps and mutual improvement, scientific and literary societies proved that the workers' well-being had been considered. The printing department alone covered 4 acres. Gardens for all, an annual flower show, prize band, boys' brigade, cottage hospital, bowling club and open-air swimming baths – there is no doubt the Farmers' Discussion Society had plenty to talk about after their visit to the land of Monkey Brand and Sunlight Soap.

GROWN WITH
HADFIELD
EXTRA SPECIA
POTATO MANUF
BY MR JAS. DOD
GREENHALG
KIRKHAM. LANC

Mr James Dodd (right) of Greenhalgh, Kirkham, telling a reporter in 1900 about the excellent results achieved after using Hadfield's Extra Special Potato Manure. Mr Dodd said: 'This is the first year I have used it and have grown the best lot I have had in my experience for 30 years. We sent off 115 loads of 240 lb each, of marketable potatoes to the statute acre, which is equal to 12 tons. Some of the roots, when lifted weighed 7 lb.' In Greenhalgh at this time Charles Day ran a laundry and Oliver Stirzaker collected income tax. Besides Mr Dodd, William Mather and Thomas Parker were market gardeners. I am told that a dish of boiled potatoes tossed in butter and fresh mint made a good dinner in Kirkham, and for tea it was 'golden syrup butties'.

A group from Kirkham Grammar School, photographed by Elliott and Fry around 1902, judging from the military uniform and the House Matron's style of dress. The drill sergeant on the left was detailed to supervise 'P.T. in the Quad', among other duties.

Ribby Road in the 1930s, where the new Kirkham Grammar School was built. Skinny Lizzie's Tuck Shop in Ribby Road was used by the grammar school boys. The notice reads: 'Teas at any time, the butter shop, pure ice cream.' Lizzie's sister worked in the mill.

Children playing in Moor Street in 1909. Mrs Norah Bennett recalled how they loved to dance to the barrel organ and longed to play it but when the man went away he 'locked it up and took the handle'. Her grandfather lent Samuel Laycock his pony and trap in return for which Samuel wrote a verse about him.

Nos 22 and 24 Moor Street damaged by enemy action on 29 September during the Second World War. Fortunately the people of Moor Street were unhurt although they were badly shaken. Other bombs and land-mines fell harmlessly around Freckleton making large holes in the ground.

A group of keen Co-operative Society officials, *c.* 1920. They were photographed at the end of every financial year. The Co-operative Wholesale Society Stores, established in the nineteenth century, was situated at 55 Poulton Street in the same building as the Co-op Picture Theatre and Appleton's wine and spirit merchant. It was then described as Co-op Central Stores and can be seen on the 1870s Kirkham photograph on page 24. Those were the days of Kirkham 'characters'. The imported Irish labourers who loved snuff and fought till the streets ran with blood were the cause of the 'Snuffy Kirkham' reputation. The uncle of Mrs Bertha Kirkham had a farm by the parish church. He lived on the main street of the town and it was his habit to drive three cows from his back garden to pasture near the railway station at Wesham, stopping the traffic as he did so. He was aged over 90 when he died and his body was conveyed to church on a farm cart.

Harold Bridges of Warton in front, wearing his father's gamekeeper's jacket and waistcoat in September 1917. Seated is Tommy Lea who taught Harold to drive. Notice the solid tyres, oil side-lamps, two-piece flat windscreen and no side doors. These were early days in the Bridges transport business. 'Inspection invited' is on the sign above the cab.

Soldiers arriving at Kirkham Railway Station on 4 August 1912. Kelly's Directory of 1901 lists the 5th Lancashire Artillery, No. 1 Battery as having its headquarters in Birley Street. The captain and honorary major in attendance was A.W. Ryland.

Little Marton Mill which dates back over 200 years to the days of the Saddle Inn. Lytham, Marton and eight nearby villages were very much part of what was once known as Windmill Land. The account book of John Whalley of Little Marton shows that Messrs Blezards, millwrights, repaired the windmill at Marton Green in August 1841 and also the windmills at Treales, Weeton and Lytham, after obtaining permission from Squire Clifton of Lytham Hall. The Whalleys were millers at Little Marton for many years but by the early twentieth century Cornelius and George Bagot had taken over. Joe Gillett of Wesham and his 18-year-old son Nicholas are among the few windmill restorers in the country. In the 1980s the Gilletts replaced two of the wooden sails on Little Marton Mill, then went on to restore the mill on Lytham Green. Mr Gillett also worked on Kirkham windmill in 1955.

The cenotaph at Kirkham on 11 November 1964. Residents were shocked to hear that month that vandals had attacked it with bricks. Councillor Mrs Alice Dawson said: 'It will either have to be cleaned or removed,' but First World War veteran Councillor Oswald Aitken opposed its removal from Barnfield and eventually the memorial was cleaned. Some residents aver that a tree was planted for every Kirkham man who died in the First World War. These can be seen alongside the track approaching the cenotaph. (Courtesy of *Lancashire Evening Post*)

Market Square in 1950, with Jackson's seed shop still on the corner. It was later swept away and a new shopping centre built overlooking the fish stones, which at today's Thursday markets are used for spreading produce on. Kirkham still cherishes this ancient site (all credit to Kirkham Historical Society and the Lord of the Manor, 'Eddie' Sergeant) where two centuries ago Thomas Tyldesley met his nephew from Bradkirk Hall before galloping off to Freckleton. In 1748 the fish stones had to be repaired. Since then they have twice been replaced and the lamp refurbished. Note here it is also being used as a signpost. The lamp replaced a market cross where banns of marriage were proclaimed, as at Poulton-le-Fylde. 'Ye Crosse' was there in Thomas Tyldesley's time as he mentions it in his diary. (Courtesy of *Lancashire Evening Post*)

SECTION TWO

Wrea Green, Freckleton, Warton

Moss Side signal-box and level-crossing in 1900.

Captain Augustus Wykeham Clifton of Warton Hall in 1905. Henry Bridges of Keeper's Cottage, Lodge Lane was his gamekeeper for fourteen years. When Henry's son Harold was born on 11 May 1900, Captain Clifton, a Boer War veteran, enthusiastically suggested his name should be Harold Mafeking Bridges, but Harold's parents would not agree. The Cliftons in Saxon times were legendary figures. Walter, son of Osbert, was recorded as Lord of Clifton and Salwick in 1160 and his heirs established the Forest of Bowland. Sir Thomas Clifton fought at Agincourt with Henry V. Richard Clifton built an oratory and the family acquired the manorial rights of Westby in the sixteenth century and more with each successive century until the twentieth when their fortunes were reversed.

The late Mrs Margaret Rowntree, alderman and twice elected Mayor of Fleetwood, seen here in the 1950s. She spent much of her childhood at Freckleton and remembered the sweetshop with its bull's-eye glass window-panes and the many varieties: 'duck and green peas, liquorice sticks, nougat, barley sugar, jap nuggets and mint imperials'. Allanson's shipyard was an attraction as her father Mr Fish was a master mariner, and so was the small windmill with 8 ft sails made by William Eccles who at one time had managed the peg-mill at Warton. In 1970 she published a book of verse recalling Freckleton around the turn of the century. Mrs Rowntree who was a member of the Fylde Board of Guardians improved conditions and increased privileges for inmates of the workhouse at Kirkham.

This occasion on Freckleton Green before the gardens were made may be the handing out of coronation mugs to commemorate George V's and Queen Mary's great occasion in Westminster Abbey in 1910. All the babies born on that day received one.

Freckleton Green with Balderstone's Mill in the early twentieth century. 'Tewitt's Invalid Stout' is advertised on a gable end (right). Coal coming from Wigan via the Rivers Douglas and Dow was unloaded at Bunker Street at a place called Coal Hill. Gardens were developed on the green in 1920.

Preston New Road, Freckleton, in 1901, now known as Preston Old Road. The smithy, which was demolished before the Freckleton Green picture was taken, is the low building in the centre, beyond the cottages on the right. In the background on the left of Preston Road is the old school.

The licensee of the Clifton Arms, Warton, in 1909 awaited the arrival of loaded wagonettes bearing customers for his strawberry and cream teas and gave them a hearty welcome. Other old photographs show this forecourt crowded with vehicles in the popular summer months.

Warton Peg Mill, built of wood in the eighteenth century, could be turned into the most favourable winds by swivelling the whole mill which was attached to a stout peg or post – hence the name peg- or post-mill. There are records of some nineteen such mills in the Kirkham area hundreds of years ago. This lovely, fragile structure is now reduced to one post and a grinding stone. Within hailing distance is the aerodrome at Warton, which commenced in May 1941 and is now the home of British Aerospace.

Warton Peg Mill in Mill Lane, 150 yd south of Lytham Road, c. 1903. It fell into disuse as weather and passage of time weakened its wooden structure and the demand for corn growing and milling faded. Originally it had a wide wooden ladder to reach the interior. Allen Clarke who visited it and wrote a book about all the windmills in the Fylde, noted that even early this century Warton Peg Mill was in an advanced state of decay. It came originally from Rufford, having been ferried across the River Ribble to Guide's House. On its central beam was carved 'P. Blundell 1717'.

Warton Bank and Moorings in the early 1900s, not far from the old Lytham Dock where traces of primeval forest were found. Peat deposits are visible below the tide line and about this time trees were exposed which gave trouble in dredging operations.

Warton church in 1906. There are four corner stones in the churchyard from an earlier building. In 1725 a chapel was dedicated to St Paul. A century later the value of Revd Thomas Henry Dundas's living was recorded as £86. All round the church lay pasture. Typical entries from contemporary trade directories for the villages around Kirkham were 26 farmers, 2 blacksmiths and 1 corn miller.

Haymaking by hand in the 1930s, a method of farming which was then dying out. Bolton Houses or Bolton House Farm as it was later referred to has much history. At the beginning of the twentieth century three-quarters of the land in Treales was pasture. Arthur Hall of Bolton House is listed in Barrett's Directory in 1924 along with forty-eight other farmers in the Treales, Wharles and Roseacre area. Innkeepers like Arthur Fenton of the Eagle and Child, one of the oldest inns in the Fylde, are included as farmers as is Robert Cowburn of Lockenstoops. At one time Lord Derby's agent lived at Bolton Houses. Squire Tyldesley hunted part of this land in the eighteenth century. In his diary he writes: 'Thence to Kirkham. Stud talking with Arthur Parker, Will Lowde and cousin Stanley. . . . As soon as day wee went to meete severall companie a'hunting. Wee earthed ye bitch ffox and tucke a cub before ye hounds alive afster running him two miles. Will Stirzaker and Hen. Kirkham and others with mee.'

Mr and Mrs Bridges with their family, *c.* 1910. The father, Henry, seated at the front, was gamekeeper for Captain Wykeham Clifton of Warton Hall. On the far right is Harold who built up the highly successful firm of carriers operating in the Lytham and Kirkham area and beyond. Reuben and Charles are the other two boys at the back. Harold was himself involved in gamekeeping, working at Salwick Hall, which in later life he bought and lived in. As gamekeeper's boy at Salwick Hall he worked seven days a week from April to December, and six days a week from 1 January to 1 April. After Christmas no hen pheasants were shot. In 1946 he was elected to Lund Parochial Church Council and was vicar's warden for ten years.

Warton Bank and Warton Brow overlooking the River Ribble in 1907. There was formerly a ford from this side of the river to Hesketh Bank on the Southport side. Because of the treacherous shifting of sandbanks there was an official guide to conduct travellers and horses safely across.

Warton Vicarage in 1906.

Warton village blacksmith, *c.* 1900. Young boys from that time remember him for the iron hoops of 2–3 ft diameter which he made for them to bowl down the village street. The village blacksmith was skilled in metalwork and could produce tools such as 'blowers', sheets of metal to help the kitchen fire to 'wuther up'.

Warton post office in 1906. The building escaped demolition in the 1940s when the American influx led to extension of the aerodrome and runway construction. Guide's House Inn and a lot of farmland disappeared as bulldozers swept in.

Freckleton cottages, dating from the early nineteenth century and seen here in the early twentieth century. Demolished in the 1950s, they were, like many others, built of handmade bricks, cobbles and wattle and daub, while the roofs were invariably thatched. At the door, the group of ladies in long pinafores forms a typical country folk gathering. In 1856 William Whiteside, schoolmaster and overseer, lived at a similar house, eighteenth-century New House Farm, situated in Snow's Lane (later Cherry Tree Road), Blackpool. Freckleton, where the village sweetshop became the National Westminster Bank, was one of the small, ancient ports dotted along the north-west coast which in their day were important. The Rivers Ribble, Douglas and Dow meet at Naze Point where Roman soldiers of the Twentieth Legion may have kept watch from this good viewpoint or commenced building a road. Flat-bottomed boats unloaded grain, slate and china clay and the remains of the quay can still be found. Schooners *Ethel, Jane, Perseverance* and *Welcome*, besides fishing smacks, were built at Allanson's Ship Yard. A group of Quakers decided to settle here because of its marsh-bound remoteness. In the records of the Thirty Sworn Men of Kirkham is: 'Received three pence and halfpenny from Quakers at Freckleton, 1702.' (Courtesy of *Evening Gazette*)

The Water Mill at Freckleton, *c*. 1920. It has fortunately been preserved as there are few known examples, although others are being brought to light. South of Marsh Gate, it probably stands on the original site of Gilbert de Singleton's water-mill in 1325, as the current there is sufficiently strong to turn the wheel.

Lytham Road, Freckleton, *c*. 1907, with a group of villagers near the shop advertising 'White Rose American Lamp oils'. Some worked in Kirkham, where there was a snuff factory, or at Selby, Jones or Moss's mills. Earlier still, some walked to Slater's Yard, Kirkham, where the first meeting house for Nonconformists was sited.

Holy Trinity church, Freckleton, which was built in 1837, seen here *c.* 1920. The old vicarage was in Preston Old Road and the new one, built in 1926, was near Clitheroes Lane. The Primitive Methodist chapel opened in 1862 on Preston Old Road and was later used as a hall. Kirkham parish church gave a pulpit to Holy Trinity which proved to be valuable when it was renovated.

The Ball family in the early twentieth century. The father, Peter, worked his apprenticeship on Burrell steam engines at Thetford. They later lived at Kirkham, Eric becoming an engineer, Isaac William ('Billy') a consultant, but Richard, the youngest, next to his mother, dying of meningitis. Peter Ball's first wife was Agnes Garlick of Treales.

Kirkham Road, Freckleton, in the 1900s was one of the streets where live eels were sold from door to door, the cry being 'Snig Fra'. Catching the eels was known as snigging and eel pie was a favourite nourishing dish in the coastal regions of the Fylde.

The Ship Inn, Freckleton, *c.* 1920, which is thought to be among the oldest inns in the Fylde. Situated in Bunker Street, it dates back to the early seventeenth century and has deep cellars which were probably used in the smuggling of contraband goods. In 1833 John Mayor was innkeeper.

Preston Road chapel, Freckleton, in a postcard series issued by B. Hargreaves of Kirkham in the 1900s. Freckleton was one of the earliest places in Lancashire where Quaker meetings were held; Joseph and Sarah Jesper, hatters and Quakers, set up a meeting house in School Lane.

Preston Road, Freckleton in the 1900s, near where Balderstone's mill provided work. Three-storey houses (right) were used for sailcloth weaving and featured a 'fruit and loom' room. John Mayor, Son & Company were sailcloth manufacturers but weaving as a cottage industry came first.

Near the Green in Freckleton, *c.* 1906. This group in boater, panama hat and cloth cap are, back row, left to right: James Parker (the licensee of the Coach and Horses Inn), Jack Snape, William Iddon. Front row: William Whiteside, William Salthouse, George Bannister. The gaitered boy round the corner wishing he could join the men is Robert Armstrong. The handmade bricks, seashore cobbles, gold watch guard and ornamental lintels all add to the atmosphere. (Courtesy of *Evening Gazette*)

A group of people from Fleetwood who travelled to Wrea Green, outside the Grapes Inn, *c*. 1901. They include from left to right: Jane Friswell, the driver from Ball's Taxis, Skipper Dilver Collinson of Cevic Steam Trawlers, Mrs Maggie Collinson, William Martland, C.H. Friswell (by lamp) who was the manager of Cevic Steam Trawlers. The Grapes Inn was known in those days as Dumpling Inn because of an annual feast of dumplings in broth. John Topham of Wrea Green became the Surveyor of Kirkham in 1860, a waterproof cape being ordered for him to carry out his duties. About the same time John Bradley, a master at Kirkham Grammar School, was appointed secretary to the Waterworks Company, with liberty to retain his situation as actuary of Kirkham Savings Bank. On 14 April 1866 the engineer from the Fylde Waterworks Company reported that Grizedale and Weeton reservoirs would be filled within one month's time.

This postcard of Wrea Green's Duck Pond sent on 5 July 1916 to May Hull reads: 'Hoping you will come back as fresh as a daisy.' The pond was then much larger and people enjoyed sitting on the grass watching the white ducks which now seem to have been replaced by mallard.

The typhoid ward, Moss Side Hospital, in the early twentieth century. The hospital was set up in 1902 to prevent the spread of virulent fevers such as typhoid, diphtheria and scarlet fever, all notifiable diseases. Known as isolation hospitals, in the Fylde these were also founded at Elswick and Fleetwood, in country areas well away from population.

John Noblett and Mrs Noblett of the Grapes Inn, Wrea Green, in 1870 were popular licensees. Always well dressed, Mrs Noblett wore a starched white apron over her black bombazine when greeting wagonette parties.

Lovers' Walk, Ribby in 1900. This was one of many favourite country rambles, an area carpeted in springtime with wood anemones and bluebells. Hugh Holmes of Lytham listed thirty-one species of flowers at Ribby in 1873. He liked to travel the area and was an interested amateur historian, not unlike the Revd Mr Thornber who wrote a history of Blackpool.

Wrea Green post office in the days of hard winters when skating on the duck pond was possible (clog irons made good skates). In the early years of this century when this photograph was taken, shooting parties in the area were joined by Dr Shaw from Kirkham and Mr Lee from St Anne's-on-Sea. There were eight main shooting days a year which involved ten beaters to flush out quarry. The lads employed were rewarded with portions of Lancashire Hotpot at lunch-time. Always well kept and still with its village pump, Wrea Green has many times won the Best Kept Village Award.

Balderstone's weaving mill in Lytham Road, Freckleton, in 1970. It was known locally as 'the cotton mill' and was demolished ten years later. Built originally around 1845, in its busy days many people were employed there. An attempt was made to reopen it after the Second World War but this was short-lived as demand declined, and the mill closed.

Thatched cottages and a windmill at Wrea Green in the early twentieth century. Peat, clay and heather, mixed and trampled by horses, together with cobblestones were used in these eighteenth-century cruck cottages. Gable ends consisted of forked tree trunks joined with a ridge-pole. In-filling was puddled clay, wattle and daub. Local handmade bricks came later.

Wrea Green Vicarage, built by Revd R.S. Stoney who took great pride in his garden, where he planted an avenue of trees. Strict but kind, whenever he passed the village shop and there was a child around he would buy it a lollipop. Sadly his only daughter died as a child on 27 December 1879.

Henry Kirkham at Bradkirk Farm, Wrea Green, in 1901, holding two horses which were regularly taken to Smithy Fold opposite where Albert Parker was blacksmith. Bradkirk Farm is now the site of old people's bungalows.

Bryning Road, Wrea Green, in the 1920s, when there was neither gas nor electricity. If you worked in the mill at Kirkham or wanted to visit the cinema, you walked there unless you had a bicycle. Some villagers persisted in using oil-lamps even after electricity arrived.

Old millstones, carefully arranged in the grounds of the restored Wrea Green windmill in the 1970s. Now fashioned into a rustic table and seats, they once had the task of grinding corn. The design of the grooves had changed little since Roman times, the millers having to dress the stones and position them in order to produce the texture of flour required.

Wrea Green village shop in 1900. 'Licensed to sell tobacco', it was the main supplier of groceries but a butcher and an ironmonger with a paraffin oil tank called once a week. The oldest inhabitant then, Tod Hull, known as 'the spirit of Wrea Green', never missed Sunday service and was not in favour of so-called progress.

SECTION THREE
Treales, Newton, Salwick, Clifton

Newton Bluecoat School in 1932.

A group of children from Wharles in 1909. Included from left to right are: James Richardson, Bill and Jack Kay (the gamekeeper's sons), Tom Ball (the tall young man), Annie Ball and Agnes Davies holding baby Alice Shorrocks. The bassinette would be a collector's piece today.

A trio of country folk at Treales in the 1920s. On either side of Annie Hesketh are Mr and Mrs Stirzaker (pronounced by the locals as The Stezzakers), who farmed at Skippool, the ancient port from which emigrants set sail in 1840 for America. The Stirzakers were regular visitors at Nook Cottage and Moorside Farm.

Treales Church Choir trip, *c.* 1909. Third from the right on the front row is Jeanetta Ball, born in 1899. Among the group (all wearing hats except the boys) are other well-known people from the village: Miss L. Sanderson, organist, Mrs Holding, and Messrs Cowburn, Birkett and Ward.

The front entrance of Clifton Hall Nursing Home in the 1980s. The hall has had a number of owners. In the autumn of 1923 Dr Hugh Riddell sold it to Sir James and Lady Florence Hacking whose head gardener, Albert Plummer, was expected to examine all skylights regularly for storm damage and to sweep the chimneys from the outside.

Elswick village, home of William Bramwell, the nineteenth-century Methodist preacher, principally belonged to Mr A. Wilson in 1921 when the population was 328. The Independent chapel built in 1753 is famous as the cradle of Fylde Methodism.

Clifton Mill, which was considered to be one of the tallest in the country, in the 1950s. Saved from total wrack and ruin, it now serves as Windmill Tavern, a restaurant and popular spot for visiting jazz bands. Ralph Slater who built other Fylde windmills was the millwright.

The sunken gardens at Clifton Hall, 1930. The line of the southern wall of the old building showed up in the dry summer of 1984. The huge cellars underneath the present Clifton Hall originate from one of the earlier halls on the site. Near to this sunken garden was a moat which surrounded the original hall.

The Lodge of Clifton Hall in 1930. The lodge was put up by Thomas Clifton in 1833, a date visible on the keystone above its large, black double doors. The old hall was destroyed by fire in 1745. From the early twelfth century, the de Clifton family held lands at Clifton and Salwick.

Miss Lizzie Gornall at Lilac Cottage, Wharles, in 1900. She kept house, tended the garden and looked after her two brothers who worked on the land. Known universally as 'a sweet and kind lady', she was very fond of children, always having fruit or toffee when they called at Lilac Cottage.

Grandpa Ball, known as 'Owd Isaac' of Isaac Ball & Sons Ltd. He hired out threshing machines, heavy roadrollers and traction engines, which were needed on roads and farms, taking orders beyond Kirkham and district. Born in 1859, Isaac came from Banks with 18s. in his pocket to find work in the Fylde. In 1881 he had a second-hand Marshall engine from which he built up his business, advised by engineer Charles Burrell. The workshop at Treales, once resoundingly busy, has nothing left but the foundry chimney and workshop next to Shorrocks's farm.

This photograph of Annie Ball of Wharles, c. 1909, gives some idea of girls' fashions: button boots, long dress with many frills and long hairstyle. Putting their hair up denoted the age of young ladies in those days. Annie attended a private school in Poulton-le-Fylde and was instructed in deportment, music and drawing.

Little Alice Shorrocks in 1912 outside Nook Cottage, Wharles, where Nelly Jenny Shorrocks was also born. Now Mrs Alice Birch, aged 85, she is the oldest resident in Ancenis Court which was built on the site of the old grammar school across from Kirkham parish church.

Nelly, from Wharles, a pretty girl in button boots dressed for Whit walking or Sunday school, in the early twentieth century. Now Mrs Gibson, she tells the amusing story of how she got her Christian names. Her mother and aunt favoured different names and argued all the way to the registrar's as to which should be chosen. When asked, 'Nelly' said one, 'Jenny' said the other, so inadvertently this little girl was given both. A Barrett's Trades Directory of this time lists Mr White's Likeness Establishment in Treales. He created tinted daguerreotypes for 7s. 6d. and may have taken this photograph.

The Preston to Lancaster Canal at Salwick in 1960. In summer this was a very picturesque spot and a favourite place to stop was by the bridge. Refreshments could be bought at the inn.

Salwick Hall in 1960. Harold Bridges earned 10s. a week here as a gamekeeper's boy during the First World War. In 1921 he purchased a Model T Ford truck and by 1966 his business had grown to a 100 vehicle 'parcels and small' operation. After selling out for one-and-a-quarter million pounds he himself became squire of the estate.

Gracemire Farm, formerly Gracemire House, Salwick, which has a 1753 datestone initialled by the Hankinson family. Attics where churns were stored had the space between the floorboards and ceiling stuffed with chaff, useful insulation in the seventeenth century. Even older, a remnant of wattle and daub wall was uncovered during alterations.

The Hand and Dagger in the 1960s. Its name was taken from the heraldic device of the Clifton family, and it was formerly the Clifton Arms, Salwick, built when the canal was being made in the late eighteenth century. The navvies who dug the canals were a tough, hard-drinking gang, frequently involved in fights and strikes.

Newholme, Preston Old Road, Newton, 1970, which has a 1639 lintel at the back door of the building bearing the initials A.R. and E.R. This could relate to Edward Robinson, a farmer. The original building had no foundations; bricks were laid and shaped to the lie of the land.

Springfield House, Clifton, in 1922. On the site of Springfield Cottage, this was the first house to be built in Clifton after the First World War, close to the site of another building demolished between 1842 and 1892. An interesting feature is the presence of long gardens on the south side as in Kirkham, possibly remnants of the ancient 'tofts'.

Bolton's Croft council estate. It was built immediately after the Second World War in rural isolation, yet close to Springfield, the factory for British Nuclear Fuels which employed many from the estate. John Harper, the manager, lived at Oakfield, a large house which in the 1920s belonged to a solicitor, Mr Dickson.

The former coach-house at Bryning Hall, originally Highgate Hall and later the Bell and Bottle, is now a private dwelling, Highgate Cottage. Bryning with Kellamergh, an undeveloped area of over 1,000 acres, consisted of scattered farms and houses, Leyland House being another of ancient origin.

Weeton Windmill photographed without its sails, *c.* 1930, was situated on a rise on the road to Thistleton and Elswick. In the early 1900s not far from the corn mill there was a meadow known as Golden Dell because of its kingcup flowers. Weeton village green was surrounded by thatched cottages, with a thatched post office and a thatched inn with a sundial. There was even a thatched dwelling where Oliver Cromwell was said to have slept for one night during the Civil War. At Weeton Lane Ends, bones and other relics of battle have been discovered.

Mrs Alice Bridges of Salwick Hall crowning the Rose Queen at Newton Bluecoat School in 1952. Clifton, Newton, Treales, Wrea Green and other villages all had annual Club Days with processions, decorated floats, prams, bicycles, sports races and a travelling fair. Crowning the Rose or May Queen was an important part of the day.

Newton Bluecoat School in 1932. The school was founded in 1707 by a yeoman farmer, John Hornbie, who had lived in Newton since 1640. His aim was to provide a good Christian training for children whose homes were poor or insecure and to fit them for work so that they could become independent, providing for themselves and generally benefiting the local community. The old building was demolished and replaced with a new school almost three hundred years later but the tradition of John Hornbie's bequest lives on. In the early twentieth century Mr Winchester was remembered as a good teacher by ex-pupils. He lived in a house adjoining the school, an even older building originally a seventeenth-century farmhouse. The sixteen-paned windows of the school with their glazing bars and stone surrounds would today be the delight of an industrial archaeologist.

The School House, Clifton, with Clifton and Salwick School, now the Lund Church Hall alongside. From Clifton to Kirkham was a schoolboy's walk of three miles. They had to go to Kirkham for a haircut which one old boy remembers cost 6d. in 1911.

Clifton Mill in the 1960s. Built by millwright Ralph Slater, it stood 90 ft high, the tallest in the Fylde, with walls 3 ft thick at the base, tapering to 1 ft. Its design differed from standard practice by having six storeys instead of five. Five millstones and five hoppers were incorporated.

The Derby Estate Tile Works, Treales, in 1893, where tiles and pipes for draining the moss lands were made. Landowners knew that the Fylde could be truly productive only if effective draining took place. Little boys found other uses for the dykes: fishing, and skating in frozen winters.

A rather damaged picture of Annie, William and Lizzie Gornall outside the thatched Lilac cottage at Wharles in 1890. The thatch, often harbouring rats and birds but wonderfully durable, was commonly replaced with corrugated iron. The dark and sometimes smoky interior usually housed old furniture: settles, a press, a deal table and a spinning wheel.

Tenant farmer Mr Stirzaker from Wharles in his garb typical of agricultural workers in the early twentieth century. Prizes in ploughing matches were often fustian breeches, leather gaiters, wool stockings or singlets. Documents from the nineteenth century reveal that tenants of farms owned by the Derbys or Cliftons were strictly controlled. '£18 per annum payable on June 5th and the tenant not to plow, break up, dig, delve in any manner or convert into tillage and meadows. If he does he shall pay the landlord £20 an acre.' Nor could the tenant 'whiten land [lime] or summer burn, take rabbits, fish, wildfowl, seashore stones, gravel or minerals'.

Jeanetta Ball at Laburnum Cottage, Wharles (opposite Shorrocks's farm) in 1912, beautifully dressed for a Whitsuntide walk. The 'rockery' behind consists of ancient roots or moss stocks. Preserved for hundreds of years, these fossilized roots and branches of trees, which came to light when the moss lands were drained, were used for many purposes all over the Fylde.

Lund Church in fields midway between Salwick and Clifton, *c.* 1936. Ancient Danes' Pad, a trackway, is traceable to the north of Lund and may be of Roman origin. There was formerly a cross in Lund village and an old font in the church, referred to by Puritans as a 'scandalous trough', was in reality a Roman altar.

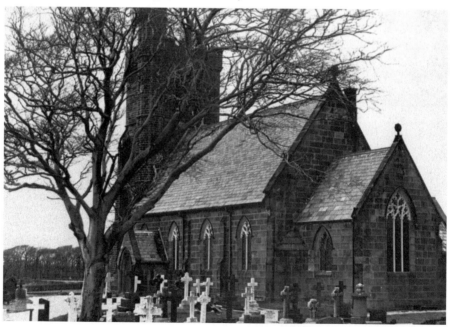

Lund Church seen here in the 1940s dates from 1825, though the foundation is older. In 1913 a cross was dedicated at Lund near Clifton Mill in memory of Edmund Birley of Clifton Hall. Children from Clifton School marched to the site with the headmaster and sang hymns in Miss Birley's presence.

A group of boys from Treales School in 1926, including Jim Shorrocks and Jack Cookson. To distinguish the many children in families it was a country habit to refer to Jenny 'John' Hesketh, Jenny 'Dick' Hesketh and Nellie 'John' Hesketh, the middle name denoting the father.

Lord Derby's shooting party at Wharles on 'Shooting Day' in the late 1890s. Dick Eccles (with shovel) and Tom Davies are the beaters. Dogs were kennelled between Carr Hill and Treales Town End. Before setting off from the Eagle and Child Inn or the Derby Arms, Lord Derby gathered with huntsmen for a stirrup-cup.

Mauretania, one of Isaac Ball & Sons' traction engines, with staff alongside in preparation for tar spraying. This was seen around Kirkham at threshing time which took place mainly in winter when bad weather often made an uncomfortable job even harder to bear. The grain had spent many weeks stooked in hassocks drying and ripening in the fields. Into the stack yard came the threshing machine pulled by the traction engine and alongside was positioned the baler. The sheaves of corn or oats taken from the stack were dropped one by one into the threshing drum until the whole stack disappeared, whereupon an exodus of rats could occur for which men stood at the ready with sticks. The grain was collected in sacks and the straw baled, much dust and chaff flying about in the process. The speed of the machines and the skill of the men working together rhythmically made for success, but everyone was glad when the job was finished.

Treales School Morris Dancers, *c.* 1910, with their headmaster, Mr Stephenson. Alice Marquis and Alice Hall are among the group. Morris dancers, harking back to a very old tradition, appeared at galas all around the district, at village Club Days, Kirkham Club Day and Poulton Festival. In this group, mob-caps or gypsy head-dresses and floral dresses are worn. Others wore white dresses, white mob-caps and black stockings, with the boys in knee-breeches, buckled shoes or clogs. The morris 'stick' was brandished in the dance. Sometimes green sashes featured, green being the colour of springtime. 'Jack in the Green' or the 'Green Man' decked with leaves and branches as a sign that winter had passed, joined in the procession. The name of this comical character appeared hundreds of years ago on some inn signs.

Nellie Ball, who became Mrs John Hesketh, on her bicycle at Treales in the early 1900s. For ladies with long skirts the 'dropped' handlebar made cycling easier. Although bloomers were more practicable garb, most women would not use them and some publicans refused to serve a lady who arrived wearing this new fashion.

Little girls ready to dance round the maypole at Treales in 1914. To keep the old custom alive, teachers worked hard training the girls and mothers saved up to provide new white dresses, white mob-caps and black stockings and shoes so that they would all be dressed alike.

An interesting stone stoop or gatepost near Newton, carved with E.R. 1654, the initials of Edward Robinson, an early landowner in Newton-with-Scales. He is thought to have been a senior officer in Cromwell's army and for a time lived at Westby Hall, now demolished. Cavaliers in 1641 forded the River Ribble at Warton or Freckleton and stole some of Edward's horses. Scale Hall Farm, Newton, also demolished, had a similar stoop but development has swept away all trace.

Treales Windmill, c. 1908, when it was 200 years old. Four storeys high and with its drying room 12 yd away, the mill once had a bank of walled earth around it, which according to local wiseacres was to prevent dampness. When a similar bank of earth at Lytham Mill was removed it led to that very trouble. Washing whitening on the surrounding hedgerows was a familiar sight. Henry Hall was corn miller at Treales in the 1920s.

A drawing of Treales Windmill which was issued as a picture postcard in the early twentieth century and also appeared in a newspaper feature. The Fishers lived at the farm nearby which is dwarfed by the four-storey brick tower mill.

The Derby Arms Inn, Treales, *c.* 1900. The name of the hamlet has changed in spelling over the years: Treals, Trayles and Treales. On 27 June 1851 a Mr Milner reported that bluetits had nested in the top of his beehive and all lived happily together, the tits raising a brood while the bees collected nectar.

Weeton, Staining, Singleton

Thistleton post office, run by Postmaster Joseph Bamber, in 1924.

Weeton Fair in the early twentieth century was held by rights bestowed under ancient charters. This was a fair for the sale of cattle and was thronged with farmers and farm labourers. For eight hundred years this noted 'Cow Fair' was held on the Monday after Whit Monday. A study of old directories reveals the predominance of agriculture and cattle rearing in the area. Kirkham organized ploughing matches. Weeton was once as well known for its bull baiting as Treales was for cock fighting. Weeton-with-Preese is recorded in Domesday Book and long ago was the head of a lordship covering Treales, Wesham, Greenhalgh, Plumpton and other hamlets, with a court held during the year. There is an ancient burial cairn and tales of 'a hairy ghost' were once part of the local folklore. The Eagle and Child Inn is said to have had continuous licensees since 1585 and also a secret cupboard. Fylde Waterworks Company whose head office was in Preston Street, Kirkham, chose Weeton as the site for their large reservoirs.

Weeton WVS Canteen & Club, during the Second World War. The ladies of the canteen did sterling war work in the area throughout the duration making snacks, drinks and meals for the troops. Although air raid sirens sounded many times the Fylde suffered little from enemy action and was considered a safe area for the evacuation of children and government records. The worst bombing occurred on 12 March 1941 at 10.45 p.m. when two land-mines were dropped on Warton creating huge craters. They smashed thousands of panes of greenhouse glass in Harbour Lane, Church Road and Bryning near the Birley Arms Hotel. It took weeks to replace the glass and exposure to frosty air killed plants.

Staining Windmill like many of Windmill Land's whirling, sailed towers was a favourite subject for artists, this painting being by a Blackpool man. Here at one time lived Mr and Mrs Rossall with their son Baden. Changing to steam-driven engines some mills suffered irreparable damage, were set on fire or fell down under the vibration. 'Rusticus', a local writer, bemoaned their fate in 1971: 'Let us try to keep the faithful old friends respectable and serving some useful purpose in their retirement.' While some did fall into rack and ruin, the Staining, Kirkham, Pilling and Wrea Green windmills are examples of those fortunate enough to have been lovingly restored and made into dwellings.

Tommy Cardwell at Weeton Camp in 1914. Weeton grew overnight from a tiny hamlet because of its population of soldiers who sought entertainment in Blackpool. Weeton, mentioned in Domesday Book, belonged at first to the Butler family and then to Lord Derby.

The Eagle and Child Fruit and Flower Gardens, Weeton, 'acknowledged to be the most pleasant drive in the Fylde, with free admission', was a change from Castle Gardens with its monkey house. Landlord Ralph Clough advertised: 'three miles from Singleton, a circular drive, excellent teas provided, wines, ales, spirits, cigars of the finest quality.'

Thatching at Thistleton, a skill which has almost died out but at one time was as important a trade as blacksmith, tinsmith, saddler, miller, innkeeper, shipwright or pavior. Very large quantities of thatch were required and, until it was outlawed, starr grass from sandhills was favoured as the most durable material.

Eccleston main street, *c.* 1900. John Ronson farmed at Kirkham i'th folds, James B. Jackson at Eccleston Hall and William H. Holmes, yeoman, at Brow Farm. Little Eccleston Hall had apertures on either side of the entrance porch designed to hold muskets for sudden attack and its windmill, burned down in 1874, was one of the oldest peg-mills.

Smiling girls at Singleton Gala Jubilee in 1935. In contrast, two hundred years earlier, Thomas Knott of Singleton wished health to King James II and death to his adversaries. The court ordered: 'He shall stand publickly at the Market Cross at the next Market Day, the seditious words he spoke being fixed on his forehead.'

The Girls' Friendly Society assembled outside Singleton School in the 1930s. As with bible classes, membership was remarkably high, 70 or 80, all joining in processions on Club Days or Whitsuntide walks. Choir trips were made locally by charabanc and further afield by train, The Dukeries and Shrewsbury being popular venues.

Lifeboatman Coxswain Wright, wearing an RNLI medal, with his wife in a bath chair and guests outside Singleton Hall at their golden wedding celebration on 3 August 1899. T.H. Miller, Lord of the Manor, built Singleton Hall, laid out the park in 1873 and later remodelled the village.

A group of parishioners with church wardens and the Bishop of Blackburn outside Singleton church, c. 1936, possibly after a confirmation ceremony. Within the church is a black oak chair reputedly used by John Milton when composing *Paradise Lost*. It was purchased by T.H. Miller in York.

The signal-box at Weeton standing dilapidated on what was the original Preston & Wyre Railway line. New methods of signalling and closure of stations has made such signal-boxes redundant.

The gardener tending the memorials to animals in the grounds of Singleton Hall in 1948. Mr T.H. Miller owned a famous stallion, Honest Tom, which won many prizes. His tombstone is carved: 'Great Honest Tom lies here at rest'. The second is: 'To the memory of our faithful dogs', and was erected by the Squire in 1905. (Courtesy of *Evening Gazette*)

Singleton Church of England School prize-winning choir, *c.* 1910. The village school built in Church Road in 1863 was owned by the Singleton Estate until 1952. The children received their whole education here until 1932, when from eleven years old they were transferred to central schools. In 1959 Mrs Jane Cowell laid a foundation stone for improvements to the school building. The School House adjoined the school grounds, the last headmaster to reside there being Thomas Dawson from 1905 to 1930. The earliest place of worship at Singleton is mentioned in 1358. By 1756 Singleton chapel was a thatched building with eaves so low they were almost at ground level, with a priest's house attached. It was all pulled down in 1806 and replaced by a square-towered church with six bells dedicated to St Anne. Alderman Thomas Miller paid £4,000 to erect the present church which was consecrated on 12 July 1860. The Revd Leonard Charles Wood, the first vicar, held the living for sixty-eight years and died at the age of ninety-two.

To be Let,
FOR THE
TERM OF THREE YEARS,
FROM CANDLEMAS AND MAY-DAY NEXT,
AT THE HOUSE OF
Mrs. Hardman, Innkeeper,
IN KIRKHAM,
ON WEDNESDAY,
The 15th of August, 1821
AT SEVEN O'CLOCK IN THE EVENING,
Subject to such Conditions as will be produced:
ALL THAT
Valuable
AND COMPACT
ESTATE,
CALLED
Thistleton House,
comprising
an excellent FARM-HOUSE, with convenient OUTBUILDINGS, of every Description,
in complete Repair,
SITUATE IN THISTLETON,
Together with the several Closes or Parcels of Land thereto belonging, containing
in the whole
56a. 2r. 28p.
Of the Measure of 7 Yards to the Perch, or thereabouts, be the same more or less,
now in the Occupation of Silvester Hodgson, who will shew the same.
For further Information apply to Miss DEWHURST, of Kirkham, (the Owner,) or
to Mr. NICKSON, of the same Place, Solicitor.

A broadsheet for the letting of Thistleton House in 1821, printed by Mr Williamson of Poulton Street, Kirkham. In that year Miss Dewhurst of Kirkham, whose solicitor was Mr Nickson, owned this valuable farm (now a luxury rest-home for the elderly). Inns, which were the first post houses in the country, also served as premises for sales. Thistleton has no mention in Domesday Book but the area Greenhalgh-with-Thistleton is listed under Greneholf, which by the thirteenth century had become Grenule. In documents of 1212 Thistilton is recorded. It was not unusual for the name of a hamlet to provide a surname for its tenants as in nearby Cornoe or Corner Row, giving Robert, Rowland and Henry Cornoe. Down the ages the spelling altered at times to Cornall. Even to this day there are Kirkhams in Kirkham.

Acknowledgements

The late Vic Baldwin • John Beardshaw • Ann Berry • Tom Betley
Stanley Butterworth • Jenny Gibson • Robert Gibson • John Gornall • Harry
Hodgkinson • Kirkham Grammar School • Lancashire Library • Brian Lund
Robert Lunt • Charles Martland • Eric Mills • North West Water •James
Plummer • Martin Ramsbottom • The late Margaret Rowntree • Tom Ruddle
Derek Timms

Picture Credits

John McGlyn: pp. 2, 47
Sheila Houghton, ATD, MA: p. 11
British Museum: p. 11
The *Evening Gazette*: pp. 17, 80, 85, 125
Ian Allan Ltd: p. 26
Lancashire Evening Post: pp. 28, 34, 57, 67, 68
Harold Bridges: pp. 43, 105
Singleton Church: p. 124